CONSTANT COURAGE

Martin Luther King, Jr.

and

Jesus Christ

TRACY EMERICK, Ph.D.

BOOKSIDE Press

BOOKSIDE Press

BookSide Press
877-741-8091
www.booksidepress.com
orders@booksidepress.com

Contents

Dedication
_____

INTRODUCTION

Are we willing to die for others to live in comfort and peace?

It takes enormous courage for one person to stand up for others and die a meaningful death. For many of us, when we speak of death, we tend to shy away and be fearful of it. We value our lives more than anything or anyone. Let's admit it. We all fall short of the kind of courage that is willing to risk ourselves for others – the kind of courage that is selfless, pure, and constant.

Our modern world has constantly shown us that we need to live our lives happily. In effect, it caused us to gain an idea of perfect lives focused on a self-centered life. The world shows that to be truly happy, we need to live contented lives – our needs and wants met.

We are bombarded by commercialism created by capitalists who constantly instilled in us the importance of self-love – *the fulfillment of our needs and wants* – knowing little that there is no such thing as *fulfilling the needs and wants* because we are humans who will never be contented. We have unlimited wants and needs, and we are being held captive in a vicious cycle of discontent.

Adding burden to this, the young ones are instilled with a mentality of YOLO (or "You Only Live Once") centered on possessing a passion and love for *living life to the fullest* by being happy and carefree because we only have one life to live.

Sadly, the young ones realize only later that to *live life to the full* does not mean living it in comfort, luxury, and perfect lifestyle. From the two personalities that this book exposes, we will learn that to truly live life to the fullest means to live a life of *constant courage*. It is a life dedicated to others, those we love; it is a quest for freedom and salvation for the people. Such does not always

1

mean a comfortable life. It is, in fact, a life filled with struggles and risks. For Martin Luther King and Jesus Christ, *constant courage* is the key to living a YOLO life, magnified by the sacrificing of their lives to make others live in comfort and peace.

In this book, I want you to open your eyes to the constant and unparalleled courage displayed by this book's two important figures: one fought for equality and justice and became the father of the civil rights movement; the other became the father of Christianity, the world's largest and biggest religion. From this book, we will discover the glaring commonalities that both personalities have, as we dig into their experiences from their younger days to the pinnacle of their lives and how they created an indelible mark on the world.

As we make parallels to these two individuals, we uncover important lessons that we can apply to our own lives and breed new knowledge that brings fresh perspectives to the readers' point-of-view. May this book also become our guide when we are lost in a generation filled with uncertainty – and know that there is hope. The patience displayed by these two personalities – Jesus Christ and Martin Luther King, will bring us an important equation for success: *Perseverance + Persistence equates to success.*

And even if things do not go our way sometimes, it is the way. We can only achieve our goals when we face failures, rejections, and intimidation. What matters most is we carry deep within our hearts the thing called *constant courage*.

By the end of this book, I want you to learn from their lives, but also come out stronger in life, wearing that cape of *constant courage* each of us needs to weather the storms of our lives. It is my hope that as you journey through the stories and lessons of this book, we come to realize the meaning of courage and re-imagine it. I hope that we see clearly a new definition of courage – not just meets the eye.

There is more to courage that its basic definition. We can unpack and uncover the essence of courage through this book. When we get to meet *constant courage* up close, we become quick to determine who are the people around us who displayed the same *constant courage*. This leads us to uncover the deeper part of ourselves and learn how we can become more like the characters of this book so we can confidently wear our own cape of constant courage.

Sit back, relax, enjoy, and be transformed. - Tracy

CHAPTER ONE

Unpacking Yourself

As long as the mind is enslaved, the body can never be free.
Psychological freedom, a firm sense of self-esteem, is the most
powerful weapon against the long night of physical slavery.
— Martin Luther King, Jr.

When we were young, we were always told to fit in.

We were always taught to become friends with others and blend in, join the bandwagon, and take part in society – valuable teachings of our childhood, imprinted in our minds and ingrained in our actions.

The problem, however, is when we grow old, we have the tendency to conform to whatever we were taught when we were young. So when the world sets the standard, we conform. Society holds a structure built by the majority. So when society treats the minority unfairly, even with the glaring presence of injustice, we are engulfed with fear to voice out and fight against it. We rather conform, take part, and join the bandwagon.

This is the society our grandparents and ancestors lived in. Before the era of Martin Luther King, black people were considered second-class citizens. There is a huge separation between blacks and whites. Whites hold the most privileged status – but not until the *constant courage* of history's most noble men and women stood in and switched the buttons that led to a new society.

4

What society dictates, we tend to conform. No one wants to be an outcast in a so-called civilized society. So when societal injustices are omnipresent, the minority has the tiniest voice. We feel the fear of non-conformity in a structured society.

2000 years ago, Jesus lived in a society that conforms to religious systems and beliefs, that if one does not conform, it is considered a crime. So when Jesus taught His teachings which were considered radical and non-conforming to the beliefs of religious and political leaders, he met a gruesome death.

Fear All Around Us

Fear has become a standard of living. Fear is instilled within us more than we know it. When we were young, we conform to academic structures because of fear of failing the expectations of our parents. When we fail to win in a certain sport or activity, we fear being rejected by people, by our colleagues. While these academic or athletic standards are set to help us become better at life – to aim higher and be the best we can become – we are taught that non-conformity can lead us to failure and misery. When we are unsuccessful, we will be excluded and rejected.

In our modern society, there is also a thing called "fear of missing out" or most commonly, "FoMo." According to the National Institutes of Health, British psychologists elaborated and defined FoMo as *"pervasive apprehension that others might be having rewarding experiences from which one is absent",* FoMO is characterized by the desire to stay continually connected with what others are doing. This breeds pressure on the current generation of young people to be abreast with the latest trends and events, rooted in fear of being disconnected.

Fear is our greatest enemy, more than ever. Fear has held us back more than we know it. Have you ever experienced being in a room of people with varying strong opinions? More often than not, we are tongue-tied and unable to speak up our own opinions because of fear. Not knowing that our opinions could change the course of the discussions. We fear that our ideas might not be good enough or acceptable enough, which causes us to just conform.

You see, fear takes away opportunities and freedoms. Fear could lead to stagnation and suppression of growth. Where new ideas could have grown, where a new set of knowledge could have sprung, we impeded its birth.

Unpacking Fears and Turning Them to Courage

Since this book talks about *constant courage*, it is important to unpack ourselves and determine our levels of courage and fear. Fear is our biggest hindrance to gaining courage. To gain courage, we need to smash the walls of fear. Here, we uncover the "baby steps" to gaining *constant courage*.

1. Know Your Fears and Know Yourself

Psychiatrist Carl Jung says, "Find out what a person fears most, and that is where he will develop next."

Fear can be a good thing when we are aware of what we fear. Awareness of our fears is the first step to courage. If fear is the greatest enemy, then we have to fight against that enemy.

If we fight that enemy, we must first know who the enemy is. Sun Tzu wrote in his famous book, The Art of War, "If you know the enemy and know yourself, you need not fear the result of a hundred battles. If you know yourself but not the enemy, for every victory gained you will also suffer a defeat. If you know neither the enemy nor yourself, you will succumb in every battle."

Do you fear speaking out your stance on any social issues? Do you fear taking a stand against the various injustices around you? Are you thinking of a new entrepreneurial activity but you fear failure? Remember that fear can hinder growth and opportunities.

Fear can either result in either *action or inaction.* Fear becomes a good thing when one responds to fear by doing what he thinks is best to prevent something from happening. Sadly, it can also result in inaction, apathy, or lack of concern. When we fear doing something courageous or noble, we miss out on the opportunity in becoming our own heroes.

2. Acknowledge Fear, Always

In Martin Luther King, Jr.'s book, "A Gift of Love," we find some of King's most powerful sermons, one of which he guides his followers on four steps to overcome fear. He writes:

"First we must unflinchingly face our fears and honestly ask ourselves why we are afraid. This confrontation will, to some measure, grant us power. We shall never be cured of fear by escapism or repression, for the more we attempt to ignore and repress our fears, the more we multiply our inner conflicts... By looking squarely and honestly at our fears, we learn that many of them reside in some childhood need or apprehension... By bringing our fears to the forefront of consciousness, we may find them to be more imaginary than real. Some of them will turn out to be snakes under the carpet."

These words from Martin Luther King give us insights that our fears may just be a result of our imaginations and thinking. Why are we afraid? What makes you afraid? When we assess these questions carefully and dig deeper into the reasons why we do, we realize fear's insignificance. The mind is where our fear resides.

Scientifically speaking, fear resides in a small region in the temporal lobe called the *amygdala.* Studies have found that the *amygdala* modulates the fear response in humans. When we start to gain consciousness of the fact that the brain is trying to generate fear and causing us to become less effective, know that we can fight it.

When we learn to control our minds by being conscious of our fears, we gain freedom. We become efficient and effective at what we do.

3. Turn Fear into Courage

Martin Luther King considers courage as a "virtue" and a "power of the mind". In his speech, King says, "We can master fear through one of the supreme virtues known to man: courage."

> *"Courage is the power of the mind to overcome fear. Unlike anxiety, fear has a definite object which may be faced, analyzed, attacked, and, if need be, endured."*

King continues, "Courage is the power of the mind to overcome fear. Unlike anxiety, fear has a definite object which may be faced, analyzed, attacked, and, if need be, endured.Courage, the determination not to be overwhelmed by any object, however frightful, enables us to stand up to any fear. Many of our fears are not mere snakes under the carpet. Trouble is a reality in this strange medley of life, dangers lurk within the circumference of every action, accidents do occur, bad health is an ever-threatening possibility, and death is a stark, grim, and inevitable fact of human experience.

Courage is an inner resolution to go forward in spite of obstacles and frightening situations; cowardice is a submissive surrender to circumstance. Courageous men never lose the zest for living even though their life is zestless;

cowardly men, overwhelmed by the uncertainties of life, lose the will to live. We must constantly build dikes of courage to hold back the flood of fear. "

In this statement, we make a clear conclusion of what courage really means and I repeat it here: It is, according to King, "*an inner resolution to go forward in spite of obstacles and frightening situations.*"

When the mind recognizes a frightening situation, it causes us to overthink. It skips the reality and visualizes the worst that could happen. In the Smithsonian Magazine, Arash Javanbakht and Linda Saab talk about fear and how to take control to gain courage:

"Fear creates distraction, which can be a positive experience. When something scary happens, at that moment, we are on high alert and not preoccupied with other things that might be on our minds (getting in trouble at work, worrying about a big test the next day), which brings us to the here and now.

Furthermore, when we experience these frightening things with the people in our lives, we often find that emotions can be contagious in a positive way. We are social creatures, able to learn from one another. So, when you look over to your friend at the haunted house and she's quickly gone from screaming to laughing, socially you're able to pick up on her emotional state, which can positively influence your own.

While each of these factors - context, distraction, social learning - has the potential to influence the way we experience fear, a common theme that connects all of them is our sense of control. When we are able to recognize what is and isn't a real threat, relabel an experience and enjoy the thrill of that moment, we are ultimately at a place where we feel in control. That perception of control is vital to how we experience and respond to fear. When we overcome the initial 'fight or flight' rush, we are often left feeling satisfied, reassured of our safety, and more confident in our ability to confront the things that initially scared us."

So, carry that torch of courage and fear not. When we learn to take control, we become a force to be reckoned with. Now that we have unpacked ourselves and learned that fear can be detached from our mental state, in the next chapters, let us define what courage truly means.

CHAPTER TWO

The Cape of Courage

But you, take courage! Do not let your hands be weak for
your work shall be rewarded.
— 2 Corinthians 15:17

When you think of the word "courage," what first comes into
your mind?

Is it a picture of an Olympic gold medalist standing on a pedestal and given the highest honors? Is it a bodybuilder flexing his strong and thick muscles to a crowd of wowing audiences? Is it a distant memory where you've shown your strength to achieve a goal? Or is it a particular person who inspired you because of that person's impact on your life brought by a courageous deed? Is it your childhood television superhero you've always wanted to be like as a child – a superhero wearing a cape saving the entire mankind from destruction?

We all have different perceptive images or icons of courage in mind. For me, I think of courage as the image of my parents who brought me into this world and whose selflessness I consider courageous. They brought me to be the best person I can be and guided me in this tough world so I can stand independently, armed with wisdom and the right amount of courage.

Courage. What is it? What does it mean to wear a cape of
courage?

It is best that we dive into the purest and simplest form of its definition, and we will expound on what each aspect means. In the *Merriam-Webster Dictionary*, courage is defined as *"the mental or moral strength to venture, persevere, and withstand danger, fear, or difficulty."* From this meaning, we discover that courage is not an action alone. It is a mental and moral strength to face to challenges of life. Read on.

First: The Mental Strength

In Merriam-Webster's definition, we first learn of courage as a mental strength. As we learned in the previous chapter, our greatest enemy is fear. We learned that fear resides in our minds. The mind alerts us of danger or risks. Immediately, our mental system injects fear into the entire mind causing our body to react to the threat or danger.

Do you still remember your first horror chamber experience? As you enter the chamber, your mind immediately injects fear even if there is really no danger at all. You know that horror chambers are only meant to scare you. It's meant to stir some fun. Your mind knows it is safe. There is no harm, right? But why do we still feel fearful of the idea?

It is because fear is all in the mind. In any situation that feels fearful, there may be possible dangers at some point, but most of those however, according to Martin Luther King are "snakes under the carpet." They are unreal, imaginary, and only a result of perception.

So how do we gain the mental strength to fight our fears? Remember the three baby steps we learned previously. To gain constant courage we follow: *Know your Fear and Yourself, Acknowledge Fear, and Turn Fear into Courage.* When we start to get acquainted with our own fears and when we start to acknowledge their presence, the more we gain the courage to face those fears.

BetterUp.com talks about mental strength as the "cognitive and emotional skill of reframing negative thoughts and adverse circumstances. Being mentally strong, or mentally tough, helps us resist both internal and external influences that weaken our self- confidence and well-being." But you might think: why is the *emotional skill* part of this definition when all we're talking here is mental strength?

> **" Success will come knocking your door when you start to shy away from negative thoughts and emotions. Be confident that you are capable of what you desire " to become.**

Know that our emotions and the mind go hand in hand. When the mind perceives something, emotions follow. It is up to us to control those emotions so that the mind will eventually cease to inject fear. This is what results in mental toughness. When your emotions and mind are aligned to combat fear, you gain mental toughness, which is the initial step to courage.

Think of the first experience you had in public speaking. Our whole body tenses, our voice shakes, we palpitate, we find it hard to breathe, and we perspire. Our body reacts to fear even if there is nothing to fear at all. You have prepared for that speech to a point that you have mastered it but your mind still tickles you and whispers to you the possibility of failure. And as the fear of failure sets in, failure now becomes more real than imaginary.

So acknowledge it, assess the situation, and know that it is imaginary. Breathe in more air, and gain mental strength. Success will come knocking on your door when you start to shy away from negative thoughts and emotions. Be confident that you are capable of what you desire to become.

Second: The Moral Strength

Courage is based on moral values. We learned that the definition clearly presents moral uprightness or strength in the resolve of achieving a venture. Therefore, can we safely say that courageous men and women should be morally strong?

The answer is yet. Moral strength or moral courage is well-defined by the American Association of Colleges of Nursing, and it goes:

"Moral courage is the ability to stand up for and practice that which one considers ethical, moral behavior when faced with a dilemma, even if it means going against countervailing pressure to do otherwise."

In essence, we learn here that courage means standing up for what is morally right. It is the practice of fighting against incorrect or unethical behaviors.

In life, we will always be dealt with unfairness. Life won't be fair for everyone. It won't be fair for all of us. We live in an imperfect world that is surrounded by evil. Let's face it: while society strives for justice, not everyone is getting a fair piece of the cake. Because perfect justice only exists when we all face our lives' judgment one day.

"
> *If courage is anchored on morality, then fighting side by side with injustice and unethical practices cannot be considered courage – even if it is meant to help others.* **"**

Because of this, it is our moral obligation to practice and hasten our individual *cape of courage* – that moral fortitude inside of us to fight against the injustices experienced by other people.

14

If courage is anchored on morality, then fighting side by side with injustice and unethical practices cannot be considered courage – even if it is meant to help others. Courage can only be acquired when it is anchored on moral uprightness. What are you standing up to? Are you standing up for the benefit of others who are experiencing injustice? or are you standing up only for your own benefit? It is therefore important to assess the motivation behind the battles that we fight. We might figure out that we are fighting only for our own selfish selves and not for the benefit of humanity.

Third: Perseverance

An important keyword in the definition of courage is *perseverance*. Perseverance, in essence, is persistence in doing something despite difficulty or delay in achieving success (Merriam-Webster).

In this definition, we are reminded that courage has an end goal. There is a target in sight. The ways and means to achieve that target courage. No matter the difficulty and delay, courage is persistent and persevering.

In life, there are times when success is delayed or difficult. We cannot guarantee the swiftness of the end results.

The life of Jack Canfield, the author of *Chicken Soup for the Soul* Series is one of the most inspiring stories of perseverance. Today, Jack is one of the best motivational speakers in the world, a professional coach, and an inspiring author who published a book entitled *"The Success Principles."*

His beginnings, however, were not that impressive. Jack and his co-author Mark Victor Hansen pitched the original *Chicken Soup for the Soul* to over 130 different publishers. With that number, one would say that it is impossible to not get one publisher.

Unfortunately, none of the 130 publishers were interested in a simple reason: no one "wants to read 100 inspirational stories."

Adding insult to injury, Jack and Mark Victor's literary agent dropped them after 100 *and more* unsuccessful pitches. But the

15

authors had a load of perseverance in them. They were determined to get the book published.

Literary agent after another literary agent, they persevered and tried their luck. They encountered difficulties along the way. But Jack and Mark Victor were confident in their work. They knew something good is coming and it only takes one publisher for them to achieve their success. Luckily, a small publisher in Florida picked up the book and published it for them.

> **"** *Perseverance will acknowledge that delay, discouragement, and difficulties are only part of the process but do not define the end-result.* **"**

Fast-forward to today, there are over 250 *Chicken Soup for the Soul Books* and over 500 million copies were sold worldwide. Imagine, if the authors dropped their books and moved on with their lives, or be discouraged by the enormous number of rejections, where would they be? Now, the book has given Jack and Mark Victor enormous fame and fortune.

Perseverance is to acknowledge that delay, discouragement, and difficulties are only part of the process but do not define the result.

Fourth: Withstand Danger, Fear, or Difficulty

Courage is also an ability to withstand danger, fear, or difficulty. When one fights for ethical and moral beliefs, one becomes a target of evil. There will be persecution, bullying, and a feeling of being an outcast. When one speaks the truth, it can cause danger, fear, or difficulty. It is up to us to be steadfast and persevere to withstand all of it. The cape of courage will help us withstand them.

Our *Constant Courage* characters in this book, Jesus Christ and Martin Luther King, are the best examples of people who withstood danger, fear, and difficulty in the quest for truth, ethics, and morals. Jesus and Martin Luther had their share of assassination attempts. In fact, from the very day Jesus was born, He already faced His first assassination attempt.

In the book of Matthew in the bible, it says that Joseph and Mary had been visited by an angel and told that Herod would attempt to kill Jesus, their son. Doing as told, they took their infant son and fled by night into Egypt, where they stayed until Herod died.

When Jesus started his ministry in his 30s, the Pharisees wanted him killed because His teachings were not considered aligned with their religious practices and beliefs. During those times, the religious beliefs are stiff, and anyone who go against the religious teaching is tagged immoral or blasphemous.

At least eight times in the Gospel accounts, people tried to seize Jesus and kill Him because of something He did or said.

In his quest for fairness, equality, and civil rights, Martin Luther King, also had his share of assassination attempts. As early as the mid-1950s, King received death threats because of his prominence in the civil rights movement. He had confronted the risk of death, including a nearly fatal stabbing in 1958, and made its recognition part of his philosophy. He taught that murder could not stop the struggle for equal rights. After the assassination of President Kennedy in 1963, King told his wife, Coretta Scott King, "This is what is going to happen to me also. I keep telling you, this is a sick society."

In the Bible, we also learn of many stories of courage and withstanding danger, fear, or difficulty. *HomeSchoolAdventure.com* publishes this inspiring story of courage on their website:

"After spying out the Promised Land, Joshua and Caleb had the entire Israelite assembly threaten to stone them for speaking the truth.

'Then the glory of the Lord appeared at the tent of meeting to all the Israelites.' (Num. 14:10)

When God spoke, the lives of these two courageous leaders in the Bible were preserved, but He decreed that the million people against them would die.

Over the next 39 years, everyone over the age of 20 died in the wilderness. Conservatively, just numbering the men, that's 15,000 funerals each year—for decades. Joshua buried his elders, his family, his peers, and his friends. Joshua surely grieved as anyone would but, rather than turn to despair, he chose to prepare the next generation for the Promised Land.

How do we know this?

At the end of their wandering, Joshua was able to assemble the entire Israelite camp for battle with just three days' notice. *'They answered Joshua, 'Whatever you have commanded us we will do, and wherever you send us we will go."* (Josh. 1:16)

Unwavering obedience and courage don't just happen suddenly. Faithfulness was modeled to the next generation, and Joshua spent years preparing them for the battles that lie ahead. Sound familiar?

Unlike Joshua, you may never have God's Shekinah glory entering your trial, but neither are the rocks filling your son's pocket intended to kill you.

Keep a healthy perspective of your hardship knowing that God will provide what you need. (Phil. 4:19) Likewise, be faithful and courageous, confident that after years of hardship and preparation. As promised, *'The Lord will do amazing things among you.'* (Josh. 3:5)"

This story teaches us that even as we face a decade of seemingly never-ending hardships, there is a purpose for all of it. Our perseverance, our persistence, and our capability to endure difficulties have a prize. Success will come knocking on our door one day, as long as we keep our eyes on the target. Wear that cape of courage!

One day, you will soon taste the sweetness of success.

In the next chapters, we will learn how our Constant Courageous men, Jesus Christ and Martin Luther King dealt with the battles through their individual capes of courage.

CHAPTER THREE

The Courage Character

We must build dikes of courage to hold back the flood of fear"
— Martin Luther King, Jr.

Courage is not only a virtue, it is a character.

While virtue is defined as a *behavior character*, possessing a character of courage is *a mental and moral quality* that becomes distinctive to an individual. Therefore, *character* goes beyond *behavior*. It is a distinct quality. So when courage becomes a part of our character, we personify it, and we can become an icon of that character in the eyes of the people around us.

For example. Close your eyes and try to envision a heroic character. What first comes to mind? I'll give you 5 seconds to do that.

Easy, isn't it? Many of us may have visualized our favorite childhood superhero characters like Superman, Batman, or Wonder Woman. Now, this time... try to envision something or someone that/who is your icon of compassion. Who or what first comes to mind? I'll give you another 5 seconds to close your eyes and think.

Who or what is it? And why is that/he/she an icon of compassion for you? In those 5 seconds, you may have visualized the most compassionate person in your life who helped you in a time of need. Someone who is always there to listen to you with all ears.

Now we come to think: Why do you visualize those specific people when we talk of a certain characteristic? Because these people have imprinted in our minds the character that they possess because *they have personified them.* Their character is shown on the outside, reflected in their actions, words, and deeds. Because of that, the "word became flesh." The word became equivalent to them. They became absolutely synonymous with the word in mind.

In this chapter, let us know more about courage or bravery and determine how we can personify them in our lives. Isn't it amazing when one person gets to imagine you when they think of courage or bravery?

Have you tried smelling a certain aroma and your mind immediately pans across a certain memory of a person or experience? That is the goal of building a *courage character.* But first, let us learn to build or personify this important character first.

Ruth Pearce talks about Bravery (a synonym of courage) as a character in *viacharacter.org.* I adopted it here for us to gain more knowledge and hopefully personify the character of courage or bravery:

Looking at the list of *24 Character Strengths*, most of them seem to lend themselves to feeling good. I love feeling gratitude, or enjoying a laugh or being kind. Who does not feel good when they feel love or loved? For those like me, who love learning or are curious, doesn't it feel good to satisfy that yearning for new facts and information?

But what about bravery?

"I wish I had more bravery," a friend said to me over the phone. "Of all the strengths, that is the one I feel I lack and should work on." It is probably a widespread thought.

Spotting Bravery

Typical images of bravery or courage are of the firefighter rushing into a burning building to save a child, or of a soldier fighting for our safety, or of someone battling disease. The fact is that we ALL use most of the character strengths to a greater or lesser extent and that includes courage. Sometimes we may just not recognize it. I think my friend is brave.

For example, she has taken a chance on a career change. She knew she needed the change, but she had no certainty it would be successful, no clear path for the future beyond taking the first step. That seems pretty brave to me.

> **Martin Luther King Jr. said, "We must build dikes of courage to hold back the flood of fear."**

As I discuss strengths, and in particular bravery with more people, I wonder if we all have a tendency to mix up being brave and courageous with being fearless? I know I have said things like "It did not feel brave to me, I was terrified!" And yet when considering courage – a blend of strengths including bravery – quotes abound that tell us that this virtue goes hand in hand with fear.

Martin Luther King Jr. said, "We must build dikes of courage to hold back the flood of fear". Mark Twain said "Courage is resistance to fear, mastery of fear – not absence of fear", to name but two.

Appreciating the Strength of Bravery

The VIA Strengths Classification defines the virtue of courage as "Emotional strengths that involve the exercise of will to accomplish goals in the face of opposition, external or internal" and comprises the strengths of bravery, honesty, perseverance, and zest.

The strength of bravery is described as "Not shrinking from threat, challenge, difficulty, or pain; speaking up for what is right even if there is opposition; acting on convictions even if unpopular; includes physical bravery but is not limited to it."

As I read those words they are not exactly synonymous with happiness or feeling good. Who wants to feel pain, threat or difficulty? Who likes to face opposition? Who chooses to feel uncertain, insecure, or vulnerable? I know I don't, and yet one of my signature strengths is bravery.

Unlike the other strengths that feel good in the moment, bravery is a character strength that may be easier to appreciate in retrospect.

Looking back on that scary presentation, or performance, the one that made you feel you would forget to breathe, the one you dreamt of for days or may even weeks beforehand, it feels good to know you went ahead despite the nerves and got through it. Maybe you got through a tough time resulting from loss or illness, and look back now and see how you have grown, or just how you kept putting one foot in front of the other despite your distress.

As you appreciate your accomplishment, THAT is when you get to appreciate bravery. If you still struggle to see your bravery, ask a friend or close family member whether they see bravery in you. Maybe through their eyes, you can come to appreciate this strength.

Reflecting on Your Own Bravery

So take a moment and look back now. Think about a time when you were scared but did it anyway, a time when one of your inner voices was saying "This is too hard" but you took on the challenge. Look kindly at yourself, or ask someone close to do it for you, because you were your best self in that moment. If it was hard but you acted anyway, that was you showing bravery! If you took on the challenge not only bravely, but also honestly, determinedly and with energy and vigor, that was you displaying courage.

Obtaining a Courage Character

Achieving that *courage character* requires a person to truly show an enormous amount of unquestionable courage. Courage beyond reproach. Courage that can withstand the challenges thrown at him.

But more than anything, it is obtaining a state of courage *mentally, spiritually, and physically.* All aspects of our being should go along when we are courageous. We never turn back. We tread on no matter what happens. Sounds too hard, right?

But achieving courage is similar to achieving life's success. The most successful people in this world started with very few steps. One small success after another bred to bigger success. No huge success came out of a big bang. It was a result of tireless, small wins that became larger with time.

I outlined here some of the important steps that I believe are a prerequisite to building small courageous wins that can affect your future and can make you achieve big courageous wins someday:

1. **Small Courageous Acts**

    We are all busy building our lives and this is why oftentimes we forget that we have to lend a helping hand to others by our little acts of courage. Start small. Giving a helping hand to our next-door neighbors when they need a helping hand is an act of small courage. When we take the step to help small businesses or entrepreneurial activities from our neighbors, that is an act of small courage that when practiced daily, can become a habit, and can lead to a larger *courageous character* in our hearts. These simple actions manifest that we have the courage to help people so they can build better lives.

    Another area where we can show our small courageous acts is when we fight injustice within our community or office. Bullying not only exists in schools. It can happen to our workspaces, too. "Power-trippers" or those in the higher professional hierarchy in the corporate world may bully or use their power to control or put an employee in a

23

disadvantageous situation to make them feel good about themselves.

Stand up for the small injustices everywhere. Become vocal even if it means losing something in effect. Know that to fight injustice, one should stand up for others to follow. It just needs one spark for a fire to burn the whole house down. Similarly, you can be an agent for positive change. Act on small injustices around you. Who knows, you can create the biggest impact in your organization.

> **When we start to gain a mentality of selflessness, when we start to determine which behaviors or actions prevent us from becoming selfless, we are clearing the path to live a courageous life.**

2. Be Selfless.

The most courageous people in this world are those who do not think of their own benefits but the benefit of the majority – or of another person.

When we start to gain a mentality of selflessness, when we start to determine which behaviors or actions prevent us from becoming selfless, we are clearing the path to live a courageous life. Courage equates to selflessness. You can never practice courage without putting others before yourself.

For the two personalities that this book exposes, Jesus Christ and Martin Luther King, Jr., both have shown enormous selflessness – and all those actions that they have shown are done for the benefit of others. Many times, they took the backseat so that others may live in freedom and salvation.

3. Find the Right Social Support

We are all influenced by the people we are surrounded with. When we are surrounded by people who love active lifestyle and are into sports, we are likely to gain that same love for the activity. When a child is fostered by a musically-inclined family, there is a high chance that the child develops a love for music when he or she grows old. This is because our environment has a strong effect on each one of us – how we think, how we feel, and how we act.

To be selfless and courageous, we have to be surrounded by that habit – and I'm saying that we should surround ourselves with people who are passionate about displaying courage every day. Be attracted and magnetized by the right circle of influence. Minds that often meet become attracted to each and result in like-mindedness.

> **"** *When we start to gain a mentality of selflessness, when we start to determine which behaviors or actions prevent us from becoming selfless, we are clearing the path to live a courageous life.* **"**

4. Enjoy the Habit of Courage

When we start a habit, we should not be dragging our feet. The love for a habit should be developed and it starts from the heart. If you are not willing to wear that cape of courage, you will never become courageous. But if you want to learn courage – with an inquisitive mind and open heart – chances are, you become the person you want to transform yourself into.

Take for instance an employee who hates his job. Most assuredly, it is too hard for him to wake up every day to do the job routine. Even stepping into the shower and brushing his teeth is a hard task, knowing too well that these preparations are done for the sake of the work he so much despised. I bet my life that such an employee will underperform, and will never lift a finger to go above and beyond his call of duty. In effect, he will never grow professionally.

Courage is like that. When our mental and physical state disagrees with developing a skill, virtue, or character, we find it hard to do the little things that can plant a seed of that skill or character within us. And even if we plant that seed within us, it will never grow. Remember, for a seed to bloom, it needs the perfect conditions to grow - an ample amount of water and sunlight to grow. However, it is not an overnight process. It is an everyday thing. If you are not willing to water that seed, even with the presence of the sun, it will die within you. It needs a whole-of-person approach.

What this means is, your whole persona should be involved and committed to building a habit, virtue, or character.

5. Embrace Failure.

This last and final small step to achieving a courageous character is simple but hard to do. Sometimes, we cannot embrace failures especially if we have done such a huge effort to put up something. When we are too invested in a certain project or undertaking, *and it fails*, we tend to wallow in sadness and despair. Worse, it can breed fears within us that hinder us from doing the same venture the next time. This can lead to missed opportunities in the future.

When we start to embrace failures, especially embracing the fact that we gain something out of the failures we commit, we build a new point-of-view of failure. There are takeaways from every failure. So even if we do not succeed in achieving something, don't worry. It's not the end of the world. We learn lessons that make us better the next time it happens.

A positive mindset, acceptance, and knowing that there is a "next time" can breed personal growth.

CHAPTER FOUR

The Father of the Civil Rights Movement, MLK

"I was a drum major for justice, peace, and righteousness."
—Martin Luther King, Jr.

A figure in the Civil Rights Movement who opened the eyes of America and the rest of the World that social injustice cannot prevail if one speaks out. This person proved that one soul can change the world forever. This is who Martin Luther King, Jr. is. An icon of activism, racial equality, and fair opportunities for all.

Born from a comfortable middle-class family, King continued the tradition of a Southern Black ministry. King's father and maternal grandfather were Baptist preachers, and so King treaded on the ministry route. His family is well-educated, and King's father had succeeded his father-in-law as pastor of the prestigious Ebenezer Baptist Church in Atlanta. Auburn Avenue, otherwise known as "Sweet Auburn," is where King's family resided. The avenue is considered to be the "Black Wall Street" as it is home to some of the country's largest and most prosperous Black businesses and Black churches in the years before the civil rights movement.

Figure 1: Atlanta, Georgia, USA - October 9, 2014: Martin Luther King Jr. Mural at the National Historic Site in Atlanta, GA

During his youth, Martin received a solid education. He grew up appreciating the love of his extended family and neighbors. However, prejudices still exist.

King never forgot the time when, at about age six, one of his white playmates announced that his parents would no longer allow` him to play with him because the children were now attending segregated schools. Dearest to King in these early years was his maternal grandmother, whose death in 1941 left him shaken and unstable. Upset because he had learned of her fatal heart attack while attending a parade without his parents' permission, the 12-year-old King attempted suicide by jumping from a second-story window.

Figure 2: Upland, CA, USA, June 5, 2020 - A person holds up a photograph of Martin Luther King at a protest of the death of George Floyd held at Merial Park in the city of Upland.

As written in Britannica.com sums up King's educational background: In 1944, at age 15, King entered Atlanta under a special wartime program intended to boost enrollment by admitting promising high school students. Before he began college, he had spent the summer on a tobacco farm in Connecticut and was shocked by how peacefully the races mixed in the North. This experience deepened his opposition to segregation laws and racial inequality.

While at Morehouse, King was mentored by the college president, Benjamin Mays, an activist committed to fighting segregation and racial inequality. Mays prodded the Black church into social action by criticizing its emphasis on the hereafter instead of the here and now. It was a call to service that was not lost on the teenage King.

He graduated from Morehouse in 1948. He later earned a bachelor of divinity degree from Crozer Theological Seminary in Chester, Pennsylvania. Ordained a Baptist minister, in 1954 he became pastor of a church in Montgomery, Alabama. The following year he received a doctorate from Boston University.

Start of the Civil Rights Movement

King was selected to head the Montgomery Improvement Association which was aimed to boycott the city's racial segregation in buses and other public transportation. Efforts eventually ended the bus segregation, sparked both love and hate from groups of people across the state.

It was in 1957 when King formed the Southern Christian Leadership Conference (SCLC). As a person gifted with the skill of public speaking, he had been active in many speakerships across the nation. His message was simple: active nonviolence to achieve civil rights for Black Americans.

King returned to Atlanta in 1960 to be with his father, the pastor of the popular Ebenezer Baptist Church. State laws at that time were still pro-segregation but King still stood against it, leading to his arrest for protesting segregation at a lunch counter. This case drew the attention of many media, including then-presidential candidate John F. Kennedy. Kennedy interceded to obtain his release.

In 1963, King organized a march on Washington, which drew more than 200,000 people at which he made his famous *"I Have a Dream"* speech. The march influenced the passage of the Civil Rights Act of 1964, and King was awarded the 1964 Nobel Prize for Peace.

In 1965 he was criticized from within the civil rights movement for yielding to state troopers at a march in Selma, Alabama, and for failing in the effort to change Chicago's housing segregation policies. Thereafter he broadened his advocacy, addressing the plight of the poor of all races and opposing the Vietnam War. In 1968 he went to Memphis, Tennessee to support a strike by sanitation workers; there on April 4, he was assassinated by James Earl Ray.

Non-Violent Activism

The long battle to achieve the goal of equal rights for black people was a fight well-fought. Fast-forward to today, black people are now secured by the laws of the land to equal rights with whites. Equal opportunities are now served. Racial equality in all aspects of society is now practiced and taught. However, this sweet taste of freedom we experience now was the fruit of a long fight. People before us, like Martin Luther King, fought hard against the odds to win this freedom enjoyed by many. But it was a long display of courage – the persistence to overcome the difficulties. Moreover, it was a result of bloodshed among those who envisioned a world of justice regardless of color.

For King, this zest to battle against racism started early as a child but there were many experiences that set Martin Luther King's heart ablaze even more. His motivation to fight against social injustice through peaceful resolution was ignited in his travel to India – his "*pilgrimage,*" he calls it.

From the early days of the bus boycott, King considers his experience in India and Mahatma Gandhi, "the guiding light of our technique of nonviolent social change". It was after the successful bus boycott in 1956 that King contemplated traveling to India where he aims to deepen his understanding of the principles of Gandhi. According to King, "India is the land where the techniques of nonviolent social change were developed that my people have used in Montgomery, Alabama, and elsewhere throughout the American South."

That same year, India's prime minister Pandit Jawaharlal Nehru came to the US. However, he was not able to meet King. Knowing King's activities in the US, Nehru inquired through diplomatic representatives concerning the possibility of King traveling to India in the future.

King had been planning to travel but there have been many interventions that stopped him from pursuing it. As King slowly recovered from his near-fatal encounter, the invitation became an opportunity for King to finally give it a go.

With the support from the Christopher Reynolds Foundation, the Montgomery Improvement Association, the Southern Christian Leadership Conference, and Dexter Avenue Baptist Church, King was able to secure his travel funds for the most meaningful and world-changing travel.

When King came to New Delhi, he discussed his perspectives on nonviolence with various heads of state: prime minister Pandit Jawaharlal Nehru and Vice President Sarvepalli Radhakrishnan.

> **Although India was rife with poverty, overpopulation, and unemployment, the country nonetheless had a low crime rate and strong spiritual quality.**

King shared reminiscences with Gandhi's close comrades, who openly praised him for his efforts in Montgomery, influencing nonviolent philosophies in global spheres of conflict. King's meetings with *satyagrahis* and his interactions with the Gandhi family reinforced his belief in the power of passive resistance and its potential usefulness throughout the world—even against totalitarian regimes. In a discussion with students at New Delhi University, King talked about the true nature of nonviolent resistance, noting that *"we are going through the most exciting and most momentous period of history."*

Throughout King's travels, he began reflecting on the similarities and differences between India and the United States. He observed that although India was rife with poverty, overpopulation, and unemployment, the country nonetheless had a low crime rate and strong spiritual quality. Moreover, the bourgeoisie—whether white, black, or brown—had similar opportunities. Upon his return from India, King compared the discrimination of India's untouchables with America's race problems, noting that India's leaders publicly endorsed integration laws. "This has not been done so largely in America," King wrote. He added, "Today no leader in India would dare to make a public endorsement of untouchability.

The coverage of the Montgomery bus boycott by Indian publications fostered King's popularity throughout the nation, welcoming supporters at every leg of the trip. "We were looked upon as brothers with the color of our skins as something of an asset," King remembered. "But the strongest bond of fraternity was the common cause of minority and colonial peoples in America, Africa and Asia struggling to throw off racialism and imperialism."

The African American and Indian overlapping minority experiences drove conversations of racialism and imperialism. Shared philosophies of liberation sparked numerous conversations as King shared his views on the race question before numerous public meetings.

King's trip to India had a profound influence on his understanding of nonviolent resistance and his commitment to America's struggle for civil rights. In a radio address made during his final evening in India, King reflected: "Since being in India, I am more convinced than ever before that the method of nonviolent resistance is the most potent weapon available to oppressed people in their struggle for justice and human dignity. In a real sense, Mahatma Gandhi embodied in his life certain universal principles that are inherent in the moral structure of the universe, and these principles are as inescapable as the law of gravitation".

The Passion for Christ

King's non-violent activism was inspired by Jesus Christ.
Like Jesus, love was King's major teaching – to treat everyone with love, even extending it to those who hate you, or your enemies.

This became the core and anchor of King's teachings, principles, and speeches. As a pastor, his love for Jesus was ultimately magnified in his everyday life. He saw that social injustice was caused by hate. Hate created a huge separation between men, which was contradictory to the teachings of Jesus.

> **"** *King's non-violent activism was inspired by Jesus Christ. Like Jesus, love was King's major teaching – to treat everyone with love, even extending it to those who hate you, or your enemies* **"**

King saw that America was not living the teachings of Jesus (teachings that were anchored on love, understanding, care, and compassion). Jesus said in His word, *"Love your neighbor as yourself"* – one of Jesus' greatest commandments that were taught to His disciples – and King definitely saw that America was not living these teachings.

Truett McConnel University published this article from 2011 on their website, *www.truett.edu*, written by Jenny Gregory, which sums up Jesus' impact on King:

Dr. Martin Luther King Jr.'s words still echo in our minds as we remember a courageous man who refused to be silent about inequality, injustice, and oppression.

Despite his political movements and his cry for equality, it was King's faith that led him to action. King was raised in the Baptist faith and would eventually co-pastor Ebenezer Baptist Church with his father, Martin Luther King Sr. Throughout his speeches and writings, he would draw frequently from his experience as a minister and his beliefs from the Bible. King was a theologian— having concentrated on Doctoral Studies in Systematic Theology and received his Doctor of Philosophy on June 5, 1955 from Boston University. The preeminence of Christ could not allow him to stay silent about inequality within the human race.

King would later become the president of the Southern Christian Leadership Conference, an organization founded by a group of black religious leaders. King was committed to non-violent protest, which stemmed from the words that Jesus spoke that we ought to love our enemies. His non-violent tactics led to the Montgomery Bus Boycott which would spark the flame that ignited the United States Supreme Court to outlaw segregation in all public transportation.

Without King's belief in Christ and faith, it is safe to say that there would have been no civil rights movement. King spoke of equality because he believed in a God who commanded to love your neighbor as yourself. His spirituality was his driving force and he adhered to Christ's words when he said that Christians must be a light in the darkness.

King's faith led him to fight. It led him to speak for the oppressed and it is his certainty that all men are created as equal, a distinctive of Baptist belief, which has influenced countless human rights movements throughout the world. He was first and foremost a man who loved God and clung to His commandments and from that stemmed King's view of the world.

Before he was titled Dr. King, before he led any political movement, he was first a reverend and a man of God. That is where he drew his strength and without his faith, there would have been no movement. In the following passage, taken from one of King's sermons, he emphasizes his belief that it is only when man recognizes his dependence on God that he can make a difference.

"Finally, this man was a fool because he failed to realize his dependence on God. (Yeah) Do you know that man talked like he regulated the seasons? That man talked like he gave the rain to grapple with the fertility of the soil. (Yes) That man talked like he

provided the dew. He was a fool because he ended up acting like he was the Creator, (Yes) instead of a creature. (Amen)

And this man-centered foolishness is still alive today. In fact, it has gotten to the point today that some are even saying that God is dead. The thing that bothers me about it is that they didn't give me full information, because at least I would have wanted to attend God's funeral. And today I want to ask, who was the coroner that pronounced him dead? I want to raise a question, how long had he been sick? I want to know whether he had a heart attack or died of chronic cancer.

> *Before he was titled Dr. King, before he led any political movement, he was first a reverend and a man of God. That is where he drew his strength and without his faith, there would have been no movement.*

These questions haven't been answered for me, and I'm going on believing and knowing that God is alive. You see, as long as love is around, God is alive. As long as justice is around, God is alive. There are certain conceptions of God that needed to die, but not God. You see, God is the supreme noun of life; he's not an adjective. He is the supreme subject of life; he's not a verb.

He's the supreme independent clause; he's not a dependent clause. Everything else is dependent on him, but he is dependent on nothing."

CHAPTER FIVE

The Light of the World, Jesus Christ

When Jesus spoke again to the people, he said, "I am the light of the world. Whoever follows me will never walk in darkness, but will have the light of life."
—The Bible, John 8:12

Jesus Christ, whose Hebrew name is *Yeshua* or Joshua in English translation, was born sometime between 6 BCE and shortly before the death of Herod the Great (as written in Matthew 2 and Luke 1:5) in 4 BCE.

The story of his birth, though remarkable, was not a very fabulous one. Jesus was born in a trough, or a manger intended for sheep and goats. He was neither a King nor a Prince, nor an heir of a high political or religious figure. All Biblical and historical accounts point that He was poor: born from Mary and Joseph, both commoners. His father was a carpenter. Bethlehem was his place of birth, an underdeveloped town, and without any industry.

The Bible tells us that there were numerous remarkable incidents in the life of Jesus Christ, but if they were all written down, it would require too many volumes, despite his short-lived ministry – that is, between two to three years.

> **" *The Bible details the most important facts about Jesus which gives us a clear picture of who He really is, how it all began, and how Christianity became the biggest religion that is today.* "**

Fortunately, the Gospel writers were able to record a great deal of literature that highlights the most important aspects we need to know about Jesus. The New Testament of the Bible details the most important facts about Jesus which give us a clear picture of who He really is, how it all began, and how His ministry developed – giving us a great source of information on the biggest and largest religion in the world today, Christianity.

Jesus' Birth

The place where Jesus grew up was complicated by religious and political forces at work in Judea. The religious forces at that time had stiff rules, and if one rejects or disobeys the religious policies, punishment awaits. The death penalty is surely a common thing during Jesus' time.

But death already followed Jesus even as an infant. In fact, Jesus would not stay long in His ancestral city because of a death threat. Shortly after His birth, Joseph and Mary brought Jesus to the temple in Jerusalem (written in Luke 2:22-38). Within months, the family would journey by night to Egypt to escape the murderous rampage of King Herod (Matthew 2:13-18).

Shortly after Jesus was born, a group of wise men (or scholars) came to Jerusalem. The scholars asked, "Where could they find the newly-born king of the Jews?" They said, "We have seen His star in the east and have come to worship him." (Matthew 2:2, NKJV). When this news reached King Herod, he sent the wise men to find Him so he could worship him, too.

But Herod was lying. Because of Herod's selfishness, and the impending risk of having a new king to replace him, he ordered his troops to kill all children below the age of two years. According to the Bible, God warned the wise men of Herod's plot in a dream, and so, they protected the child Jesus.

This caused Jesus and His family to evade Bethlehem or Jerusalem and instead found a temporary home in Nazareth, a city of Galilee.

Jesus as a Child

The book of Luke 2:40 gives us a summary statement describing Jesus' development from infancy to puberty: "*And the Child grew and became strong in spirit, filled with wisdom; and the grace of God was upon Him.*" Jesus, as a child, had wisdom greater than His age.

Jesus experienced a natural maturing process like any growing boy, but He was especially endowed with a kind of mental and spiritual wisdom far more advanced than the young men His age. When it came to grasping the Word of God and spiritual principles, He was exceptional – *He had an extraordinary gift.*

One of the accounts written in the Bible was when young Jesus was missing after a festival. Mary and Joseph went back to Jerusalem to search for Him, and later, they found Jesus in the temple.

Jesus was found in the temple involved in serious discussions with some of the learned teachers of the law in Jerusalem, "both listening to them and asking them questions" (Luke 2:46).

It was told that these young men or scholars were astounded by Jesus' questions and responses, reflecting His intelligence and spiritual maturity. He showed an astounding grasp of deep theological topics which prompted scholars to sit down and listen to Him. In the book of Luke, it says, "All who heard Him were astonished at His understanding and answers." That scenario exemplified the divinity and wisdom of Jesus even as a child.

The Biblical accounts state that Joseph and Mary were bewildered by their Son's behavior and more surprisingly, the seeming lack of appreciation for the anxiousness He had caused.

The Bible tells us that Mary asked his son: "*Son, why have You done this to us? Look, Your father and I have sought You anxiously.*"

But the young Jesus responded to His mother's inquiry by saying, "*Why did you seek Me? Did you not know that I must be about My Father's* business?"

The Harms of His Teachings

Jesus' ministry started with his 12 disciples: Peter, Andrew, James, John, Philip, Bartholomew/Nathanael, Matthew, Thomas, James son of Alphaeus, Simon the Zealot, Judas the Greater, and Judas Iscariot are names that have been closely associated with the Jesus' teaching since the earliest days of Christianity.

During Jesus' ministry, He met numerous persecutions and oppositions. But like our other *Constant Courage* guy, Martin Luther King, Jesus, too, never had the word *"quit"* in mind.

OpenTheBible.org posted this article written by Meredith Hodge that talks about the heavy opposition Jesus faced as He spread His ministry. This gives us an idea of the amount of courage Jesus had in facing each of them:

"I opened God's Word with a heavy heart, feeling the burden of opposition.

A friend had recently attacked my character due to a difference in ethical beliefs. Stunned and hurt by this, I quickly recognized my unpreparedness in facing this attack. Thankfully, the Holy Spirit prompted me to seek the Lord and the truth of his Word.

I opened my Bible and was led to Hebrews 12:3, which answered my prayer for relief: "Consider him who endured such opposition from sinful men, so that you will not grow weary and lose heart."

Six Ways Jesus Faced Opposition

Jesus, the Man of Sorrows, experienced opposition far worse than my situation. But in His eyes, it's not relevant, for all who call on his name receive the same power and ability to face opposition. In studying and understanding the character of Jesus revealed in Scripture, I felt thoroughly equipped to face this challenging situation by mirroring Christ's response.

When we are antagonized or provoked, our first step should always be to ask the Holy Spirit to guide our hearts, minds, and words. 1 Peter 3:15 instructs us to "give an answer to those who ask," and Colossians 4:6 instructs us to speak graciously "so that [we] may know how you ought to answer each person."

1. Jesus exposed motives.

In Mark 3, we find Jesus approaching a disfigured man in the synagogue. Verse 2 explains, "[The Pharisees] watched Jesus to see whether he would heal him on the Sabbath, so that they might accuse him." Mark tells of Jesus challenging them by responding, "Is it lawful on the Sabbath to do good or to do harm, to save life or to kill?" (v. 4). Manmade rituals enforced by the Pharisees had made God's Law joyless, and Jesus exposed their prideful and judgmental hearts.

2. Jesus sought peace.

When Jesus is arrested, in fear and protection, Peter cuts off the ear of the high priest's servant. Instead of affirming this act of violence, Jesus commands peace:

"Put your sword back in its place. For all who take the sword will perish by the sword. Do you think I cannot appeal to my Father, and he will at once send me more than twelve legions of angels? But how then should the Scriptures be fulfilled, that it must be so?" (Matthew 26:52-54).

Not only does Jesus condemn this behavior, but displays His loving nature by healing the man's ear (Luke 22:51).

3. Jesus applied Scripture.

In Matthew 9, Jesus is found "reclined at a table in the house" with tax collectors and sinners (v. 10), which stirred up controversy amongst the Pharisees.

They ask his disciples, "Why does your teacher eat with tax collectors and 'sinners'?" (v. 11). How does Jesus respond? "It is not the healthy who need a doctor, but the sick. But go and learn what this means: 'I desire mercy, not sacrifice.' For I have not come to call the righteous, but sinners" (vv. 12-13, NIV). Jesus used Hosea 6:6, the very scripture the Pharisees preached, to challenge their hardened hearts.

Later in Matthew 12, Jesus uses the same scripture from Hosea to challenge the Pharisees: "If you had known what this means…you would not have condemned the guiltless" (v. 7).

4. Jesus prayed.

As Jesus awaited his impending suffering and death, he stepped aside in isolation to pray. Opposition caused Jesus to feel sorrowful and troubled, overwhelming his soul to the point of death (Matthew 26:36-38). Jesus, fully God yet fully man, still needed His Father. Three times in Gethsemane, Matthew says He "fell with his face to the ground and prayed, 'My Father, if it is possible, may this cup be taken from me. Yet not as I will, but as you will'" (vv. 39, 42, 44).

Similarly, in the Gospel of John chapter 17, Jesus prays for Himself, for his disciples, and for all believers. As his impending death and resurrection approached, He prayed for salvation and for the Father's glory as He awaited this fulfillment (vv. 1-5). He lifted up his disciples in prayer for physical and spiritual protection, unity, the full measure of his joy, obedience, and sanctification (vv. 6-19). Jesus prayed for all believers, that they may hear His message, believe, unite, evangelize, and be saved (vv. 20-25).

5. Jesus remained silent.

When Jesus is arrested and faced with the Sanhedrin looking for false evidence against him, they question him. "Are you not going to answer? What is this testimony that these men are bringing against you?' But Jesus remained silent" (Matthew 26:62-63, NIV). Jesus was aware of their bias, hostility, partiality, and their past history of twisting his words. His silence demonstrated how undeserving they were of a response. Though Jesus later responds in truth to their questions, he is still accused of blasphemy, declared worthy of death, spit in the face, struck with their fists, mocked, and provoked (vv. 64-68). Yet amidst the turmoil, he chooses silence.

6. Jesus loved.

As Jesus languished on the cross, he didn't counter his accusers with insults, cursing, and retaliation—nor did he use his power to inflict pain. His submissive silence was a divine response from the nature of an almighty, all-powerful, sovereign God in the flesh—an example for all his people to follow. He withstood excruciating agony as long as he could so the door would be open to salvation, including for his enemies. Jesus forgave the thief on the cross hanging next to him who had earlier hurled insults at him, yet repented in his last moments (Luke 23:39-43). He prayed for the forgiveness of the very people who were crucifying him: "Father, forgive them, for they do not know what they are doing" (Luke 23:34, NIV). Even those responsible for the crucifixion had forgiveness available to them in love from the Lord.

Can you imagine the results had Jesus responded differently under opposition? Lives wouldn't have changed, hearts wouldn't have been transformed, and his beloved wouldn't have been welcomed into his kingdom.

Equipped for Opposition

In following the tactics used by Jesus in the face of his opponents, this encounter with my friend ended in a manner I was not expecting. Though not immediately, our relationship was healed and elevated to a new level of intimacy and love—a true miracle of the Lord's mercy and grace. Be encouraged, dear friends; though opposition in this world is inevitable, we can stand equipped under our Savior's example and by his life, rising victoriously over it.

This article clearly draws an important conclusion: Oppositions can result in danger, fear, and difficulty but through the teachings and stories of Jesus, we learn the right way to respond to opposition: to show our good motive, our peace. We need to apply truth and prayers. At times we might need to stay silent. But above all, we display *love*.

In the next chapters, let's learn how the lives of Martin Luther King and Jesus Christ became the most important icons of courage. What anchored their courage, and what brought them to become symbols of courage across the world?

CHAPTER SIX

The Cape of Love

'Love your neighbor as yourself.'

In the earlier chapters, we learned that wearing the cape of courage means withstanding danger, fear, and difficulty.

In the stories we exposed, however, we learn *how* we should withstand those dangers, fears, and difficulties. To personify the qualities of Martin Luther King and Jesus Christ, we need to wear two capes: the *Cape of Courage* and the *Cape of Love.*

The *Cape of Love* shown by the two personalities of this book is what transcended their mission to great heights. For *Courage* to remain *Constant*, love is an unalienable and inseparable ingredient.

Love is the greater motivation and inspiration for the nonviolent activism of Martin Luther King. Love is the greater motivation and inspiration for the peaceful dissemination of the message of healing and peace for Jesus Christ. Both personalities encountered extreme opposition and persecution but they never faltered to spread their teachings and hope anchored by the element of love. The two great men knew so well that when they achieve their goals *with love*, they will enlighten an estranged world and bring forth love to the hearts of the people who follow them.

But what are the elements in the *Cape of Love*? In this chapter, let us look into each of our *Constant Courage* men, and see how they used their individual *Capes of Love* as they bring forth their message and mission.

Martin Luther King's *Cape of Love*

Most of us respond to *hate* with *hate*. *Opposition* is often met with *opposition*. But Martin Luther King wore not only the *Cape of Courage* but a *Cape of Love*. This combination of both courage and love not only overturned a nation but also became a legacy story for the world to learn and understand that we can respond to hate with love, and still come out successful at it.

A golden lesson for generations that we can learn from Martin Luther King: When we start to wear our *Cape of Love* in facing the opposition that surrounds us, we magnetize the opposition into understanding our noble intentions and motivation.

When Martin Luther King was rained over with hate and opposition, he used the words of Jesus which were anchored on love. He was arrested numerous times because of crimes committed against the repressive laws.

A few months after the bus boycott, in fact, King's home was bombed which prompted blacks to retaliate against the white community.

But King invoked the words of Jesus: "He who lives by the sword will perish by the sword. We must meet violence with non-violence. We must meet hate with love."

During King's first arrest (in 1956), King stood firmly with courage, saying, "I was proud of my crime. It was the crime of joining my people in a non-violent protest against injustice. It was the crime of seeking to install within my people a sense of dignity and self-respect. It was the crime of desiring for my people the unalienable rights of life, liberty, and the pursuit of happiness. It was above all, the crime of seeking to convince my people that non-cooperation with evil is just as much a moral duty as cooperation with good."

Later that time, King founded the Southern Christian Leadership Conference (SCLC) which trained leaders in meeting *violence* with *non-violence*. King intensified his most important weapon against the enemy – *love*. Using Gandhi's approach, King became more convinced that love and peace were the only effective methods at that time. There was no way retaliation and bloodshed can bring out his desired outcomes.

> **"**
> *Seeking vengeance is one of the most common reactions or responses. Human as we are, we have the innate qualities of pride and ego. We respond to hostility with hostility.* **"**

In an interview with King, he said, "We feel also that one of the great glories of American democracy is that we have the right to protest fair right. This is a non-violent protest. We are depending on moral and spiritual forces using the methods of passive resistance. Even if we have to receive violence, we will not return violence.

Even with those pronouncements, in 1958, King was again met with extreme opposition through violence. At his *"Stride Toward Freedom"* book signing event, King was stabbed by an assailant. But this kind of violence was met with love. As a Christian, Martin Luther King used the words of Jesus in every attack against him. Clearly, he wore the two capes needed to obtain *constant courage* – the *Cape of Courage* and the *Cape of Love*.

King, in his own words, magnified his goodness of heart and the intention to be brothers with the whites by saying, "An eye for an eye leaves everybody blind. The time is right to do the right thing." At 6:05 P.M. on Thursday, 4th of April 1968, Martin Luther King was shot dead while standing on a balcony outside his second-floor room at the Lorraine Motel in Memphis, Tennessee. It was the news that shook America and the world. And even as King died due to violence, his message of peace reverberated even more.

Despite the end of his life, his words continued to live in the hearts of many.

Jesus Christ's Cape of Love

How do we react when we face hostility?

Seeking vengeance is one of the most common reactions or responses. Human as we are, we have the innate qualities of pride. Our egos get the better of us. We respond to hostility with hostility. We normally do not allow ourselves to sit there and not take revenge for the bad things people do against us. But here, we learn that Jesus used a very unique method in approaching hate and hostility: *bless your enemies.* The book of Luke 6:27-28 magnifies this intention of Jesus: "But to you who are listening I say: Love your enemies, do good to those who hate you, bless those who curse you, pray for those who mistreat you."

Therefore, retaliation through hostility is not the way for Jesus. What are the hostilities and rejections that Jesus faced? Let's look at an article by *InterserveUSA.com* which outlines the different oppositions that Jesus faced:

"I think the opening six chapters of Luke give us a good idea [of the oppositions He experienced].

In his first chapters, Luke shows us that Jesus encountered a gradually increasing level of opposition. The opposition begins in Nazareth where Jesus' own townspeople resent him and even try to kill him (4:16-29). With no explanation given, Jesus is able to walk right out of that danger and goes on his way (4:30). This encounter in Nazareth serves as a portent, preparing us for Jesus' rejection by his own people and his demise on the cross.

In this vein and from this point onward Luke shows us that Jesus encountered an increasing level of opposition to his ministry. It grows out of his interaction with the paralytic (5:17-26). The opposition increases when Jesus eats at Levi's house along with a large crowd of tax collectors (5:29-32) and also when Jesus heals the man with a withered hand (6-11). Luke points out the heightening of the tension by describing the reaction of the scribes and Pharisees. They were filled with fury.

Immediately after this, Jesus chooses the 12 disciples. Yet, even in the choosing of the twelve, Luke keeps the theme of opposition alive by concluding the selection with the dark comment that Judas, one of the twelve insiders, will eventually betray Jesus. In this way, Luke fully establishes the story of Jesus as one of growing opposition."

> **"** *Jesus not only taught His disciples to meet hate with love, but to build a somewhat non-traditional mindset to hate: To consider opposition, repression, and attacks as* **"** *"blessings."*

Opposition: A Blessing

Like Martin Luther King, Jesus met a great deal of opposition even if He has done great miracles for the poor as he journeyed through the land. But knowing all the persecutions Jesus encountered (and what His disciples will encounter), there is an *extremely different approach* that Jesus taught His disciples. Jesus not only taught His disciples to meet *hate with love*, but to build a somewhat non-traditional mindset about hate:

To consider opposition, repression, and attacks as "blessings".

The proof of that can be read in the book of Luke Chapter 6: *"Then he looked up at his disciples and said: Blessed are you who*

50

are poor, for yours is the kingdom of God. Blessed are you who are hungry now, for you will be filled. Blessed are you who weep now, for you will laugh. Blessed are you when people hate you, and when they exclude you, revile you, and defame you on account of the Son of Man. Rejoice in that day and leap for joy, for surely your reward is great in heaven; for that is what their ancestors did to the prophets."

In these verses, Jesus speaks of great rewards that await those who experience repression and hate. But he continues: *"But woe to you who are rich, for you have received your consolation. Woe to you who are full now, for you will be hungry. Woe to you who are laughing now, for you will mourn and weep. Woe to you, when all speak well of you, for that, is what their ancestors did to the false prophets."*

Here, we learn that Jesus' disciples were taught to rejoice over the suffering they encounter, and in contrast, those who oppose Jesus' disciples will face the consequences.

Interserve USA, a Christian organization continues dissecting how Jesus reacts to opposition:

"However, dishing out a just dessert to these tormentors is not God's desire. This is why Jesus' disciples are to demonstrate a completely different attitude toward suffering and respond in love and in kindness to their tormentors. This is also why Jesus immediately goes on to say that his disciples are to love their enemies (6:27-36). And this is why Jesus winds up by saying that his disciples are to be merciful as their Heavenly Father is merciful.

Jesus knows that this is so counterintuitive. It will be only natural for the tormented to tell their tormentors how wrong they are. This is why Jesus tells his disciples that when they are tempted to do this, they are to pull the log out of their own eyes and leave the speck alone in their tormentors' eyes.

Responding like Christ to the opposition is not easy. But think - it wasn't easy for Jesus either. The Gospel of Luke teaches us that Jesus didn't live on his own power. He depended upon the power of the Spirit. In this way, Jesus showed us the way we can live up to the standards He set: by absolute dependence on God's Spirit."

Cape of Love and Its Effect to Humanity

Looking at how Martin Luther King and Jesus Christ lived and responded to criticisms, bashing, opposition, hate – *name it* – we realize the great similarities that both personalities have.

You see, King patterned his non-violent protests to Jesus' teaching. This kind of non-violent protest freed the black communities from being second-class citizens. We come to think: What would have happened if Martin Luther did not apply Jesus' words and life to his resistance? What if Martin Luther King resorted to counter-violence instead of peace and love?

> **"** *Tyranny and violence, as we know it, always fail in consistency and continuity. But love, anchored on goodness, humanity, and hope, will always succeed.* **"**

And what if Jesus resorted to violence as He spread the message to the world – the same methods applied by the world's most influential tyrants? But history teaches us that no matter how widely successful the world's most vicious and notorious tyrants were, their successes were short-lived: Adolf Hitler, Mao Zedong, Joseph Stalin, Pol Pot, Leopold II, and all others. Their lives taught us that cruelty, tyranny, and evil may bring some sort of success in their quest for influence, but they fail miserably in our measurement of success – *the influence that goes beyond generations.*

But look at our *Constant Courage* personalities – Jesus and Martin Luther King – who used *love* as the core of their teachings. Their life messages still remain alive and relevant today. Their messages, in fact, are now the foundations of the laws of our land to bring forth peace and harmony in many countries, including the United States.

In my other book, *"Extreme Entrepreneurs: Steve Jobs and Jesus Christ,"* I explained how Jesus and Steve Jobs placed a dent in the world through their entrepreneurial ingenuity. But most importantly, in Chapter 10 entitled *Jesus Christ*, I wrote the glaring contribution of Jesus to the laws of the United States:

...This was a recognition of Jesus's teaching that God within us gives us unalienable rights. In other words, the right to life liberty, and the pursuit of happiness are not granted by the government but by God to every individual; thus, negating the authority of governments over the governed. But to make sure that the US government would never have the ability to subdue the governed, this body of minds in the late 1700s put together the governing rule book, the US Constitution. The preamble reads:

We the People of the United States, in Order to form a more perfect Union, establish Justice, insure domestic Tranquility, provide for the common defense, promote the general Welfare, and secure the Blessings of Liberty to ourselves and our Posterity, do ordain and establish this Constitution for the United States of America.

The constitution then goes into the branches of government and the expectations of each branch. But the most important to the individual became known as the Bill of Rights, that are contained in the first ten amendments. The following are those amendments that, if read in the context of protecting the individual, illustrate the genius of the authors of the document. Read the following in the context of a person living in Jesus's time to gain a perspective of how Jesus's teachings were manifest in these writings. These individual rights, framed in the love for the individual, define what the government cannot do in order to protect the individual from oppression, thus ending the fear of government.

Looking at the influence of Jesus Christ and Martin Luther King, vis-à-vis all other thought-leaders who resorted to hate than love, we make a conclusion:

Tyranny and violence, as we know it, always fail in consistency and continuity. But love, anchored on goodness, humanity, and hope, will always succeed. Even as the messenger dies an earthly death, the message lives on – a legacy that goes beyond generations. Martin Luther King and Jesus Christ did not only create a better world to live in, but they also changed the rules of the game. They brought new, humane perspectives that continue to change society, organizations, countries, and kingdoms until today.

How do we show that cape of love every day? Remember that if our goals and desires are anchored on love, our success will always be long-term. Success, triumph, even power, is sweet when it is inspired and motivated through the Cape of Love.

CHAPTER SEVEN

Withstanding the Long Struggle

"But I say unto you, Love your enemies, bless them that curse you, do good to them that hate you, and pray for them which despitefully use you, and persecute you"
—The Bible, Matthew 5:43–44

Now that we have learned how Martin Luther King and Jesus Christ dealt with the many oppositions against them, we realize the amount of patience and courage they have in order to remain persevering in their individual missions. True and *constant courage* requires one to truly withstand the tests of time – the long struggle to achieve one's goal.

But how can we embody this kind of extreme perseverance? The kind of persevering quality that can withstand the struggles and remain patient despite the seeming inefficacy of our actions or solutions?

Many of us experienced the struggle of putting so much effort into a specific project, business, or endeavor. And you can probably relate that sometimes it comes to a point when it feels like it's going down the drain, or it is not producing our expected results. Why does this happen? Because success comes not only with *sets of triumphs* but with *sets of failures*, too. Tasting sweet success means tasting first the bitter reality that we have to doubt ourselves sometimes, we have to be pressed hard, and we have to be shaken to bring out the best in ourselves.

When studying our two *Constant Courage* personalities, we pick up so many insights and new perspectives that can transform those doubts we have over ourselves. When we are dealt with difficulties and opposition, we often doubt our capabilities. But here, we learn that if we remain steadfast in our goals, we can achieve greater things.

Let's take a look again at the great lessons that all of us could pick up from Martin Luther King and Jesus Christ: to meet hate with non-violence, constantly strive for peace instead of violent retaliation, and let justice roll by itself. Be patient that someday, justice will prevail. Know that things will eventually fall into place as long as you remain constant in upholding peaceful resolutions, *with love at the center of it all.*

In this chapter, we will learn that achieving success is a long struggle. And those struggles are harder than we know them. Jesus and Martin Luther King did not achieve success in a snap of a finger. No, Martin Luther wasn't a magician. And Jesus isn't a superhero character.

Instead, they took the yoke of struggle as they hold on to their faiths. There were numerous moments of persecution (that if one has very little faith, one would call it quits). It's so easy to decide to drop everything when we struggle too much. But here, we learn that our two courageous men did not falter in their faith. *Their struggles even boosted their will to move onward.*

Long Struggle for Peace

As Martin Luther King strove for justice and equal rights, he was met with violence not only from whites. Amazingly, he met violence and resistance from the very community that he fought for – the blacks. While there were white men and women standing *with* and *for* him, there were blacks who were impatient and angry toward King.

After the death of President John F. Kennedy, President Lyndon Johnson was sworn into office. President Johnson ensured the passage of the Civil Rights Act of 1964 – the most important civil rights legislation signed into law since the 15th Constitutional Amendment of 1870. It guaranteed the right to vote to all male citizens regardless of race, color, or previous enslavement. The new federal law of 1964 prohibited discrimination based on color, race, religion, or origin – in public schools and employment.

While this amendment became vital for the equal rights and freedom of blacks, many parts of the country still experienced discrimination and violence against the black Americans. Thus, the passage of new federal law did not mean the struggle was over. Bombings and killings of blacks were still rampant. Some groups of black people felt the need to resort to the same violence against the whites.

But King pressed on by saying, *"We will not substitute one tyranny for another. Black supremacy is as dangerous as white supremacy."* Groups of black people were becoming very impatient with King and the absolute freedom from violence. A new generation of black leaders was now emerging and was eager for a more decisive change – including taking up arms and expressing their anger through violence.

In 1964, King experienced violence for the first time, directed against him by the blacks as he had many times by whites. He was assaulted by a black Muslim. An increasing number of blacks disbelieved in his way of non-violent activism. Throughout the nation, many resorted to violent retaliation. But King pressed on with his mission with what he called *"non-cooperation with evil."*

King indeed proved himself right. The constant violent retaliation caused greater violence than ever before. King persevered to continue his message of peace: *an eye for an eye leaves everybody blind.* Even up to his death in 1968, King remained steadfast in his call for peace.

But the most significant turn occurred after King's death: his death energized the Black Power Movement. Black Americans felt even more distrustful of white institutions and America's political system. Membership in the Black Panther Party and other Black Power groups surged. Local organizations grew into national networks. The number of black soldiers in Vietnam supporting Black Power increased dramatically. Polls revealed that some white Americans expressed support for King's goals, but many remained unmoved.

Still, the Civil Rights Movement that Martin Luther King established became the beacon of light: that to achieve a great nation, we should come together – as one – for a greater America. Other than this, while it is true that the battle is fought long and hard, there is light. Martin Luther King's life teaches us that achieving a goal peacefully is not an easy road. And definitely, there are no shortcuts. But it is the only way to go – be peaceful, be kind, be loving for a greater reward awaits. Consistency in courage, persistency in kindness.

Today, while it is a fact that racism can still happen any time, the majority of America has now opened its eyes to the real meaning of truth, justice, and equality for all. Without King's life, mission, and teachings, the freedom and equality that we enjoy today may not be at hand.

The Prince of Peace

The patience and peace upheld by Martin Luther King can be likened to Jesus Christ. After all, King patterned his non-violent activism to Jesus' message of peace. This peaceful and loving quality of Jesus inspired Martin Luther King to take a different route to freedom – despite receiving violence, *we respond with love*.

RivalNations.org writes about a scenario in the Bible when Jesus met his oppressors face to face. This displays Jesus' peaceful character:

"After Jesus' arrest, when Jesus was asked by Pilate, the governor of Judea, *'So you are a king?'*, Jesus responded in a roundabout way. Pilate understood the concept of the *king* to be a powerful, coercive, violent earthly ruler. Since Rome already had one of these, Caesar Tiberius, all other self-proclaimed kings were considered impostors or revolutionaries trying to overthrow Rome. Jesus would affirm that He is indeed a king, but first, He had to **redefine kingship**. Jesus said that His Kingdom is *'not of this world,'* and that if His kingdom *had* been of this world, His followers *'would fight to prevent my arrest...'* (John 18:36).

Christ's remark to Pilate thus suggests that a distinctive characteristic of all who belong to His Kingdom, and tha distinguishes His kingdom from the kingdoms of this world, **is that they do not fight,** even when they would be considered justified to do so."

This kind of peaceful character is what inspired Martin Luther King to bring his message of equal opportunity and anti-discrimination through non-violence. *Standing your ground in peace* is the most effective way to achieve resolution – and to achieve your mission too.

It is extremely difficult, however, for us to extend love to those who hate us, as we learned in the previous chapters. We are humans born with the seed of sin within us. We are born with a seemingly *built-in* anger and madness within us especially if we are placed in a very disadvantageous state. When we meet injustice and oppression we respond to anger and frustration even as children.

It is innate for a child to respond in anger when a child deals with injustice. Remember the time when your playmates take away your toy or when you are cheated on by your playmates? I'm pretty sure that as a child, you were furious.

But remember, it is our goal to embody the qualities of Martin Luther King and Jesus Christ who became so successful in bringing their messages out to the world through love. With this in mind, how do we deal with our enemies every day when our systems have built an innate quality of fury and anger?

> **"**
>
> # Jesus' teachings of love and peace shattered the walls that divide God and mankind. **"**

This is what Christ came on earth for. Christians believe that Jesus came to bring peace to a mankind stricken with sin and immorality. Sin created a huge wall that divides man and God. But because of Christ's presence on earth and His death on the cross, peace came forth which crushed those walls. There is a penalty for sin through the blood of Christ. Galatians 1:4 of the New Testament Bible says, "The Lord Jesus Christ is the One *"who gave Himself for our sins so that He might rescue us from this present evil age, according to the will of our God and Father."* He gave Himself for our sins; He paid the penalty and provided atonement.

Other than this, Jesus' teachings of love and peace shattered the spiritual walls that divide God and mankind. Jesus now broke the old perspective of God as someone *"too far away"* from humanity. Through these radical teachings which were centered on love, he was oppressed and hated by people, which eventually led for Jesus Christ's death on the cross. Despite this, Jesus remained steadfast in His mission to bring forth love and peace. In his dying words, he still manifested his peaceful nature as written in Luke 23:34: *"Then Jesus said, 'Father, forgive them; for they do not know what they're doing...'"*

Personifying Peace

When we deal with our enemies in a peaceful manner, we not only change the course of the conversation to our advantage, we change the response of our enemies, too. Kenneth Copeland Ministries talks about *"5 Ways God Promises to Deal with Your Enemies"* on their website:

"I have many aggressive enemies; they hate me without reason. They repay me evil for good and oppose me" (Psalm 38:19-20). Do you ever feel the way David did here?

People speak against you for no reason, betray you, or try to keep you from success. Enemies are something each of us has to deal with in this life, and they can try us in every possible way.

Our natural response to enemies is often to fight back, get even, put them in their place, or demand justice. We can even find ourselves distressed as we try to figure out why they are against us in the first place. The next thing we know, it's consuming all our thoughts and causing us torment.

When you obey Jesus and respond to your enemies with love, prayer, forgiveness, and blessing, you take yourself out of satan's line of fire and make room for God to handle justice as only He can. You don't have to worry about your enemies. God says He will handle them on your behalf. How? Here are five ways God promises to deal with your enemies.

1. **He will bring everything hidden into the light.** Enemies can be sneaky. They will say cutting remarks to you that no one else notices, threaten you when others aren't around, or try to quietly cheat you out of money, opportunities, or relationships. Even so, there is One who sees everything that is done in secret, and He says, "Nothing is secret that will not be revealed, nor anything hidden that will not be known and come to light" (Luke 8:17, *NKJV).*

2. **He will avenge you.** That desire you have for justice? That comes from the One in whose image you were

61

created. He is the God of justice, and He loves justice. It's good to want justice in the world, but when you try to get it for yourself, you've put yourself in His place. Romans 12:19 says, "Never avenge yourselves, but leave it to the wrath of God, for it is written, 'Vengeance is mine, I will repay,' says the Lord" *(ESV)*.

Under THE BLESSING, God has promised to deal with our enemies. Gloria Copeland says, "The Lord shall cause your enemies who rise up against you to be defeated before your face. This is THE BLESSING; this belongs to you. They will come against you one way but flee before you seven ways. When you are under the curse, you run from your enemies, but under THE BLESSING, they run from you." You may not see it firsthand, but you can count on Him to carry out what He has promised.

3. **He won't let enemies succeed against you.** Your greatest enemy has come to steal, kill and destroy. And he doesn't work alone. He'll use other people to carry out his plans. Sometimes, it even seems like those plans are succeeding. Isaiah 54:17 says, "No weapon formed against you shall prosper, and every tongue which rises against you in judgment you shall condemn" *(NKJV)*. So, if you have people trying to sue you or harm you in some way, you just walk in love toward them and stand on that scripture. Faith has no fear.

4. **He will prepare a table before you.** When you're walking in love and in obedience to God's Word, no matter who comes against you, they can't stop the blessings God has in store for you. Satan uses people to try and get us into offense. He knows if he can get us in strife and out of love, we're out of position to receive the blessings of God. So, stay on the love line and don't budge. No matter how much wrong is done to you, forgive, love, and pray. Then,

declare and receive His promise to prepare a table before you in the presence of your enemies (Psalm 23:5).

5. **He will help you defeat the real enemy.** At the end of the day, you might think your enemy is your co-worker, your neighbor, or your mother-in-law, but the true enemy is the one pulling all the strings. Ephesians 6:12-13 tells us that we do not fight against flesh-and-blood enemies but against evil spirits. Most of us know this truth, but it takes a constant reminder when flesh and blood are right in front of us causing so much trouble! God has given you all authority over the enemy. So, when he tries to send people your way, rebuke him, send him packing, and remind him that he must go back where he belongs—under your feet!

> **"** *So, to withstand the long struggle, there is one way to deal with it – keep on wearing the cape of constant courage and constant love.* **"**

These are five ways God *promises* to deal with our enemies. Remember, like any other promise, they require obedience on our part. If we are unforgiving and unloving toward our enemies, the promises are off the table. If we are worried, trying to take justice into our own hands, or gossiping about the situation—no deal. Stay in obedience, and let God deal with your enemies.

--

So to withstand the long struggle, there is one way to deal with it – keep on wearing the cape of *Constant Courage* and *Constant Love.* There are great rewards for those who wear those capes as long as they remain grounded in their beliefs.

I believe that it's about time for all of us to re-assess our individual lives and see where we can improve ourselves in terms of our level of patience to achieve our goals. When Martin Luther King was questioned and pressured by some black community about why he kept on espousing non-violent protest despite the continuing violence thrown against the blacks, he simply said "Be patient". King never gave in to the pressure from outside. He stood firm by his belief that non-violence is the only way.

What are the things in our lives that we are standing firmly on, but are causing us to doubt because of the pressures from the world around us? Are we being influenced by the people around us to negate from what we firmly believe in?

CHAPTER EIGHT

Power of Words:
Martin Luther King

*"Free at last, free at last. Thank God Almighty, we
are free at last."*
—Martin Luther King, Jr.

Words have power.

This is what Jesus Christ and Martin Luther King proved in their
years of spreading their teachings of love and hope. Both lived very
short, however. Jesus died at the age of 33, while King died at the age
of 39. But despite the shortness of their lives on Earth, they placed
a huge dent in the universe through their words which influenced
generations, built foundations for our laws, brought freedom to the
enslaved, and crushed the walls that divided the world.

In this chapter and the next, we will look back at the powerful
words that our two *Constant Courage* personalities left which
transformed the world, as we try to decipher their innermost being
through their words. These words displayed – without a doubt –
their amazing *Constant Courage* character that is worth emulating.

Martin Luther's "I Have A Dream"

For Martin Luther King, his motivation was a *dream* – a dream that one day, his fellow Black Americans will no longer live as second-class citizens. In one of the most remarkable days of American history, on the steps of the Lincoln Memorial on August 28, 1963, King delivered his most unforgettable speech, *"I Have a Dream"*. This speech became the most famous speech of King, and became one of the most iconic speeches of all time.

"I am happy to join with you today in what will go down in history as the greatest demonstration for freedom in the history of our nation.

Five score years ago, a great American, in whose symbolic shadow we stand today, signed the Emancipation Proclamation. This momentous decree came as a great beacon of hope to millions of slaves, who had been seared in the flames of withering injustice. It came as a joyous daybreak to end the long night of their captivity. But one hundred years later, the colored America is still not free. One hundred years later, the life of the colored American is still sadly crippled by the manacle of segregation and the chains of discrimination.

One hundred years later, the colored American lives on a lonely island of poverty in the midst of a vast ocean of material prosperity. One hundred years later, the colored American is still languishing in the corners of American society and finds himself an exile in his own land So we have come here today to dramatize a shameful condition.

In a sense, we have come to our Nation's Capital to cash a check. When the architects of our great republic wrote the magnificent words of the Constitution and the Declaration of Independence, they were signing a promissory note to which every American was to fall heir.

This note was a promise that all men, yes, black men as well as white men, would be guaranteed the inalienable rights of life liberty, and the pursuit of happiness.

It is obvious today that America has defaulted on this promissory note insofar as her citizens of color are concerned. Instead of honoring this sacred obligation, America has given its colored people a bad check, a check that has come back marked 'insufficient funds.'

> **"**
> *Now is the time to lift our nation from the quicksand of racial injustice to the solid rock of brotherhood.* **"**

But we refuse to believe that the bank of justice is bankrupt. We refuse to believe that there are insufficient funds in the great vaults of opportunity of this nation. So, we have come to cash this check, a check that will give us upon demand the riches of freedom and security of justice.

We have also come to his hallowed spot to remind America of the fierce urgency of Now. This is not time to engage in the luxury of cooling off or to take the tranquilizing drug of gradualism.

Now is the time to make real the promise of democracy.

Now is the time to rise from the dark and desolate valley of segregation to the sunlit path of racial justice. Now is the time to lift our nation from the quicksand of racial injustice to the solid rock of brotherhood.

Now is the time to make justice a reality to all of God's children. I would be fatal for the nation to overlook the urgency of the moment and to underestimate the determination of it's colored citizens. This sweltering summer of the colored people's legitimate discontent *will not pass until there is an invigorating autumn of freedom and equality. Nineteen sixty-three is not an end but a beginning. Those who hope that the colored Americans needed to blow off steam and will now be content will have a rude awakening if the nation returns to business as usual.*

There will be neither rest nor tranquility in America until the colored citizen is granted his citizenship rights. The whirlwinds of revolt will continue to shake the foundations of our nation until the bright day of justice emerges.

We can never be satisfied as long as our bodies, heavy with the fatigue of travel, cannot gain lodging in the motels of the highways and the hotels of the cities.

We cannot be satisfied as long as the colored person's basic mobility is from a smaller ghetto to a larger one.

We can never be satisfied as long as our children are stripped of their selfhood and robbed of their dignity by signs stating "for white only."

We cannot be satisfied as long as a colored person in Mississippi cannot vote and a colored person in New York believes he has nothing for which to vote.

No, no we are not satisfied and we will not be satisfied until justice rolls down like waters and righteousness like a mighty stream.

I am not unmindful that some of you have come here out of your trials and tribulations. Some of you have come from areas where your quest for freedom left you battered by storms of persecutions and staggered by the winds of police brutality.

You have been the veterans of creative suffering. Continue to work with the faith that unearned suffering is redemptive.

Go back to Mississippi, go back to Alabama, go back to South Carolina go back to Georgia, go back to Louisiana, go back to the slums and ghettos of our modern cities, knowing that somehow this situation can and will be changed.

Let us not wallow in the valley of despair. I say to you, my friends, we have the difficulties of today and tomorrow.

I still have a dream. It is a dream deeply rooted in the American dream.

I have a dream that one day this nation will rise up and live out the true meaning of its creed. We hold these truths to be self-evident that all men are created equal.

I have a dream that one day out in the red hills of Georgia the sons of former slaves and the sons of former slaveowners will be able to sit down together at the table of brotherhood.

I have a dream that one day even the state of Mississippi, a state sweltering with the heat of oppression, will be transformed into an oasis of freedom and justice.

I have a dream that my four little children will one day live in a nation where they will not be judged by the color of their skin but by their character.

I have a dream today.

I have a dream that one day down in Alabama, with its vicious racists, with its governor having his lips dripping with the words of interposition and nullification; that one day right down in Alabama little black boys and black girls will be able to join hands with little white boys and white girls as sisters and brothers.

I have a dream today.

I have a dream that one day every valley shall be engulfed, every hill shall be exalted and every mountain shall be made low, the rough places will be made plains and the crooked places will be made straight and the glory of the Lord shall be revealed and all flesh shall see it together.

This is our hope. This is the faith that I will go back to the South with. With this faith we will be able to hew out of the mountain of despair a stone of hope.

With this faith we will be able to transform the jangling discords of our nation into a beautiful symphony of brotherhood. With this faith we will be able to work together, to pray together, to struggle together, to go to jail together, to climb up for freedom together, knowing that we will be free one day.

This will be the day when all of God's children will be able to sing with new meaning 'My country 'tis of thee, sweet land of liberty, of thee I sing. Land where my father's died, land of the Pilgrim's pride, from every mountainside, let freedom ring!'

And if America is to be a great nation, this must become true. So let freedom ring from the hilltops of New Hampshire. Let freedom ring from the mighty mountains of New York.

Let freedom ring from the heightening Alleghenies of Pennsylvania.

Let freedom ring from the snow-capped Rockies of Colorado.

Let freedom ring from the curvaceous slopes of California.

But not only that, let freedom, ring from Stone Mountain of Georgia.

Let freedom ring from every hill and molehill of Mississippi and every mountainside.

When we let freedom ring, when we let it ring from every tenement and every hamlet, from every state and every city, we will be able to speed up that day when all of God's children, black men and white men, Jews and Gentiles, Protestants and Catholics, will be able to join hands and sing in the words of the old spiritual, 'Free at last, free at last. Thank God Almighty, we are free at last.'"

Martin Luther King Jr., delivered this speech to a massive group of civil rights marchers gathered around the Lincoln Memorial in Washington DC. The March on Washington for Jobs and Freedom brought together the nation's most prominent civil rights leaders, along with tens of thousands of marchers, to press the United States government for equality. The culmination of this event was the influential and most memorable speech of Dr. King's career. These words of Martin Luther King influenced the Federal government to take more direct actions to realize racial equality more fully.

Texas A&M Today posted dissects this brilliant speech of Martin Luther King on their website, written by Lesley Henton, from the Texas A&M University Division of Marketing & Communications. This review very well dissects why the speech became one of the world's most popular and moving speeches of all time:

"Dorsey, associate dean for inclusive excellence and strategic initiatives in the College of Liberal Arts, said one of the reasons the speech stands above all of King's other speeches – and nearly every other speech ever written – is because its themes are timeless. 'It addresses issues that American culture has faced from the beginning of its existence and still faces today: discrimination, broken promises, and the need to believe that things will be better,' he said.

Powerful Use of Rhetorical Devices

Dorsey said the speech is also notable for its use of several rhetorical traditions, namely the Jeremiad, metaphor-use, and repetition.

The Jeremiad is a form of early American sermon that narratively moved audiences from recognizing the moral standard set in its past to a damning critique of current events to the need to embrace higher virtues.

'King does that with his invocation of several 'holy' American documents such as the Emancipation Proclamation and Declaration of Independence as the markers of what America is supposed to be,' Dorsey said. 'Then he moves to the broken promises in the form of injustice and violence. And he then moves to a realization that people need to look to one another's character and not their skin color for true progress to be made.'

Second, King's use of metaphors explains U.S. history in a way that is easy to understand, Dorsey said.

'Metaphors can be used to connect an unknown or confusing idea to a known idea for the audience to better understand,' he said.

For example, referring to founding U.S. documents as 'bad checks' transformed what could have been a complex political treatise into the simpler ideas that the government had broken promises to the American people and that this was not consistent with the promise of equal rights.

The third rhetorical device found in the speech, repetition, is used while juxtaposing contrasting ideas, setting up a rhythm and cadence that keeps the audience engaged and thoughtful, Dorsey said.

'I have a dream' is repeated while contrasting 'sons of former slaves and the sons of former slave owners' and 'judged by the content of their character' instead of 'judged by the color of their skin.' The device was used also with 'let freedom ring' which juxtaposes states that were culturally polar opposites – Colorado, California and New York vs. Georgia, Tennessee and Mississippi."

--

Without a doubt, the speech of Martin Luther King changed the direction of America. 5 years after his speech, King was assassinated in his hotel room. Despite his death, the words still remain alive and continue to be a blueprint for equality and social justice in America today.

CHAPTER NINE

Power of Words: Jesus Christ

"For God so loved the world that He gave His only begotten Son..."
—Apostle John

Jesus Christ's words, like those of Martin Luther King, both garnered positive and negative reactions from different strata and organizations of the community.

Jesus Christ's words angered the high religious officials in His time, but brought joy to many of those who were considered "sinners" – the tax collectors, the thieves, adulterers, and those considered "filthy" in society. These people thought their situations were helpless.

We must note that in the past, sinners were considered unclean by religious leaders and even so by political groups. If Martin Luther King fought bravely for black Americans, Jesus fought courageously for the sinners. But why the sinners? Isn't Jesus concerned with the righteous and clean people who follow all of God's commands?

Jesus Transformational Words

Jesus' words stirred mixed reactions – defiance, anger, hatred, joy, and acceptance. Like Martin Luther King, when Jesus started His ministry, He encountered both condemnation and support from people.

In the early parts of Jesus' ministry, He was accused of being friends with the sinners and being blasphemous. In my other book, *"Nifty Neighbors: Mister Rogers and Jesus Christ",* I outlined the reason:

The Pharisees, a Jewish social movement during the time of Jesus, were known as the "separated ones." Pharisees follow a strict avoidance of gentiles, persons considered unclean, sinners, and Jews who are less observant of the law. Laws were very much important to the Pharisees.

The Pharisees aim to extend the practice of their religion to the everyday lives of people. They were motivated by a zeal for Judaism.

The basis of their teaching was not only the written law (called Torah) and the prophets but also various oral traditions of detailed observances and practices which they themselves inherited.

The positive aspects of the work of the Pharisees were: they extended the practice of religion beyond the temple, into the lives of ordinary people; and they wished to remind people of the presence of God among them and to call them to respond to his presence by observing certain religious practices.

No wonder that when Jesus performed his miracles and spread his parables and teachings, the religious leaders thought it to be blasphemy and a violation of the religious laws. Jesus' teachings and actions were radical. Jesus cared for the sick, dined with the sinners, and talked to a tax collector, the adulteress, and the prostitutes. He was one with the unclean and the judged groups of people.

Therefore, Jesus' ways and teachings seemed to have sparked a radical movement in His time. He was shifting the course of religion by teaching God's word, but allowing forgiveness and mercy anchored on love, raising the eyebrows of religious leaders who felt threatened by his popularity.

But Jesus' words were transformational. In many instances, He clarified that He came for "the sick": Jesus said, "It is not the healthy who need a doctor, but the sick. (Matthew 9:12)

His radical teachings of *"loving the sinners"* transformed the perception and beliefs of people, especially their hearts by giving hope to those who felt hopeless of God's forgiveness. Religious traditions in Jesus' time invoke that only the righteous can be one with God, thus creating a huge wall for those who were willing to seek God but feel unrighteous, unholy, or undeserving of His forgiveness.

> *" And now abide faith, hope, love, these three; but the greatest of these is love," as written in 1 Corinthians 13:13 "*

Love Beyond Religion

While there are countless teachings of Jesus that were written in the Bible – lessons about fear, courage, hope, tact, money, evil, obedience, life, death, eternity, and so on – Jesus' strong core message remains the same.

Love was the very essence of Christ's teachings to humankind. "And now abide faith, hope, love, these three; but the greatest of these is love," as written in 1 Corinthians 13:13. In another verse, it was said: One of them, an expert in the law, tested him with this question: 'Teacher, which is the greatest commandment in the

Law? ' "Jesus replied: 'Love the Lord your God with all your heart and with all your soul and with all your mind. ' This is the first and greatest commandment.

The word "love" was mentioned 714 times in the Bible.

Jesus was more concerned with love than any other thing in the world; teaching his disciples that love springs from God who is selfless and is reaching out His hand to the sinners, only if one believes. This teaching, however, angered the religious leaders who strongly believed that religious teachings are necessary for that is "the will of God."

Even as Christ's earthly body died on the cross, love was still the essence of His death. In the book of Romans 5:6-8 it says, "You see, at just the right time, when we were still powerless, Christ died for the ungodly. Very rarely will anyone die for a righteous man, though for a good man someone might possibly dare to die. But God demonstrates his own love for us in this: While we were still sinners, Christ died for us.

Christ's courage is rooted in love. Love is what fans the fire of courage within Jesus so that He could spread His message to the world. That message (the words) became the power that transformed people and elevated Christianity into becoming the biggest religion or belief – even after 2000 years!

CHAPTER TEN

So What?

Now that we have compared the lives of Martin Luther King and Jesus Christ, we ask ourselves: So what? How do these stories affect me as an individual and how can I make use of their stories as I live my life? How can these stories still be relevant to my life, my children, and the future generations?

First, know that everyone of us has a Cape of Courage. We can make use of this by taking simple and little acts of courage in every day. Any small acts of courage can be a good starting point. Let's wear those *Capes of Courage* every single day as we encounter people: in our homes, in our workplaces, and in our communities. Any injustice that we see and feel around us, we should now feel responsible for it – because we cannot let apathy breed oppression and violence. When we are apathetic, the more we encourage the evil to reign over our communities. That tiny voice within us should go out there and speak out, and not be afraid to voice out what is right.

However, we need to also wear the *Cape of Love.* Because courage can sometimes go overboard and resort to violence. When our courage is not anchored on love, it can result to evil. We should blend the right amount of Courage with an extreme amount of love to truly embody the two courageous personalities that this book discusses.

Second, knowing the facts that this book exposes, we now acknowledge that the freedoms that we enjoy today are attributed to these two personalities who placed their lives on the line – *with such extreme courage* – for the generations to enjoy a life of liberty. We may not be believers of Martin Luther King or Jesus Christ, it cannot be denied that their contribution to our society is enormous. Their courage and love have changed our future (and the world's future) for the better.

Martin Luther King's role in the civil rights movement cemented not only lasting equal opportunities for black Americans but also created a lasting *rule of harmony* between whites and blacks, of migrants, of naturalized citizens, and those born of different ethnicities. Harmony amidst differences. Love amidst color. Humanity over everything. Most importantly, it became a *blueprint for other nations* who may encounter the same racial inequality issues. The civil rights movement is now a model for the world.

In the same way, Jesus Christ's *message of love* also cemented an everlasting rule for America and the world – that to live in harmony is to live a life that is concerned for the welfare of others because we are all equal. As I wrote in my book *"Extreme Entrepreneurs: Steve Jobs and Jesus Christ"*:

It took about 1,800 years for Jesus's teachings about love and *God within* to be adopted by a governing body – a government created by minds from the thirteen colonies that became to be known as the United States. Several kindred souls bonded to create the oppressed colonies' position statement that would end England's rule, the Declaration of Independence. The opening statement set forth a unified set of beliefs as the strategy to create a new government:

"We hold these truths to be self-evident, that all men are created equal, that they are endowed by their Creator with certain unalienable Rights, that among these are Life, Liberty and the pursuit of Happiness."

This was a recognition of Jesus's teaching that God within us gives us unalienable rights. In other words, the right to life liberty, and the pursuit of happiness are not granted by the government but by God to every individual; thus, negating the authority of governments over the governed. But to make sure that the US government would never have the ability to subdue the governed, this body of minds in the late 1700s put together the governing rule book, *the US Constitution.*

We have the presence of Jesus in our every day life more than we know it. His teachings governs, and will continually govern us ahead. In fact, it is the teachings of Christ that led Martin Luther King to achieve his great achievement for this nation.

As a Baptist minister, Martin Luther King espoused non-violence because Jesus did. King espoused love because Jesus did. King espoused peace because Jesus did. King also took courage because Jesus did.

King kept on moving forward, pressed on, and never gave up. Why? Because Jesus did.

It's amazing to think that a man born 2000 years ago continues to inspire and lead this world with His message of love, and becomes a guiding light to our current generation beset by problems of self-centeredness. We are living in a generation that lacks the courage to fight for what is right and often fails to act in love and kindness when there is a need to. We need to shift that now. And it starts with *you.*

Know that the man named Jesus Christ who was born 2000 years ago is still truly alive until this very day. With the magnitude of his influence on our world today, Jesus' word lives. And as the Bible says, *"and it dwelt among us."*

Indeed, knowing those truths we discussed, He truly does.

Now, I am confident that as you close this book, you are more than ready to wear that cape of *Constant Courage.* Wear it well.